Vera V. Ross-Holley

Come Back, Julia!

A Tale of Love, Loves Lost, Abuse, and the Come Back!

iUniverse, Inc.
Bloomington

Come Back, Julila!
A Tale of Love, Loves Lost, Abuse, and the Come Back!

iUniverse books may be ordered through booksellers or by contacting:

iUniverse
1663 Liberty Drive
Bloomington, IN 47403
www.iuniverse.com
1-800-Authors (1-800-288-4677)

ISBN: 978-1-4620-5879-2 (sc)
ISBN: 978-1-4620-5880-8 (e)

Printed in the United States of America

iUniverse rev. date: 10/17/2011

This book is dedicated to the memories of Bernice and Daniel Ross, Julia's parents. Daniel Ross left impressions upon Julia that helped carve the person that she became. He gave his very last dime to his children, grandchildren, and friends. Julia was equally generous.

He worshiped the ground that his children walked on, and Julia worshiped the ground that her children walked on. He did not back down from anyone, and neither did she. Bernice knew that, no matter what, Julia (Tyding) was going to be there for her, come what may! If you messed with Bernice, you had a fight on your hands … a fight that you could not win!

Contents

Thanks to my husband, Lettie Holley, Sr., for encouraging me.

Thanks to Angel and Jersie, my cousins, for keeping the lights on!

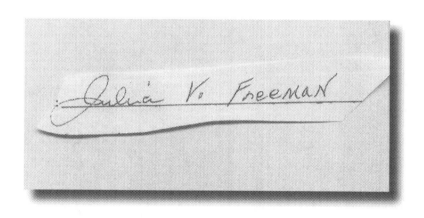

Julia and the Loves of Her Life!

Wow! Mother and Daughter!

Introduction

Come Back, Julia! is a story about a beautiful woman whose life changed when doctors diagnosed her behaviors as symptoms of Alzheimer's disease. When you encounter someone who has Alzheimer's disease or dementia on the street, in the grocery store, in the mall, or in a crowded hospital emergency room, it may be hard to understand why the person keeps repeating the same thing over and over.

If, in reading this book, you get a better understanding of Alzheimer's disease and how it impacts not only the life of the person with this disease, but also his or her family, then the work that went into penning this account will be well worth it. The purpose of this book is to bring about a better understanding of the disease and make people realize that there is a real person whose original personality is locked inside of a brain that has become tangled and mangled, a brain that just does not work the way it used to, hiding all of the curveballs that life may have dealt the person, whose whole life seems to have come to a screeching halt.

As you read about Julia, you will see a woman who lived life to the fullest when she was younger. This is a story about a mother, a wife, a daughter, a cousin, an aunt, a niece, a friend, a grandmother, and a great-grandmother. She occasionally went to church on Sundays. She worked to take care of her children. She loved "cabarets," New Year's Eve parties, going to the beach, and going "down the country." She wore shorts and high heels and lots of make-up, and she dyed her hair. She let her grandchildren take baths in the rain and shop in the Goodwill stores to buy any toys their hearts desired. She took in the homeless and children who were motherless and fatherless. She washed the cancerous sores on the legs of her dying grandmother when it was just too difficult for anyone else to do. She was ready to fight anyone who disrespected her mother. She adored her father. She would give her last dime to a stranger. Her daughter tries to put it all into words from the beginning to the *beginning*.

When you finish reading this story, you will be asked to make an observation based on the contents of this text. Was Julia's condition really Alzheimer's disease, or is this a story about the abuse of an elderly person who lost control of a life that was weighing her down, and because of the abuse, caved in when she thought that all hope was gone?

This book takes you into the life of a real person, and the intended audience is the millions of families who may have loved ones who look and act like Julia. Since reading about the experiences of others has always helped me, I hope that Julia's story will help you, the family member, or you, the caregiver, manage a very difficult life with someone who will need you around the clock. This person will need you to take care of almost every aspect of his or her life. Will it be impossible for you to do? You decide!

One morning, when Julia woke up, nothing mattered in the whole world. Only her heart remained the same. Even her eyes had lost their smile. Come Back, Julia!

As you read about Julia, you will find that before dementia (Alzheimer's disease) took control of Julia's life, she was a working woman who raised two of her four children as a single parent. She spoke perfect English—including the use of expletives. She possessed beautiful penmanship, believed that a woman must wear high heels to be considered dressed, taught her sons to fight, held two full-time jobs, and lived what she considered a normal life. So what happened?

In this attempt to find out what happened, I take you, the reader, on a journey into the life of Julia. I have explored all possibilities; maybe she had a nervous breakdown because of abuse or the weight of her world on her shoulders, or maybe it is really Alzheimer's disease.

When you finish reading this journey into Julia's life, you decide, and whatever you decide, make sure you use the lessons learned from Julia's life.

CHAPTER 1
A Woman in Control

I clearly remember being Julia's only child, even though I was not the oldest or the only. Journey with me down memory lane as I tell Julia's story.

I was so angry; I just could not understand why my brother had to live with us. In my room, as I talked to myself, I remember saying, "He is so stupid with his dark self!" The summer months were over, and Herbert, my brother, had to come home from the country to live with us. He made me sick, trying to act like my father.

My ranting and raving went on for months after my brother moved back to Baltimore. I just could not understand why he had come back from visiting my cousins from "down the country." I remember that my great-grandmother had passed away, but he could have stayed down there with my cousins. They liked him. I didn't. Well, at least Julia was happy.

We moved from my grandparents' house to our own apartment and it took some time to get used to being in a small apartment with my stupid brother. He really did watch over me when Julia went to work, but he kept trying to tell me what to do: *Don't talk to boys,* and *you gotta be in the house by seven o'clock,* and *don't get off the steps,* and *go in the house,* and, and, and!

My God, he was a nuisance. I knew that he was only doing what Julia told him to do. I should have told her that he made me sit on the front steps while he ran through the alley with his stupid friends. I should have told her that he got on my nerves and that he made me sick! He kept checking to make sure that I stayed on the stupid steps with some little old ladies who made me sick, too. They were always trying to get into my mother's business.

"Where does your mother work?" they asked.

"How come she ain't never home?" the really nosey one asked.

It isn't her business, and anyway, "ain't" is not a word in the English language with her stupid self! I thought. *She is so stupid.* Julia said you do not put two negatives in one sentence. I should have told the stupid thing that!

"How old is your mother? She looks really young," the short one asked.

Even when I answered all their stupid questions, they still had new questions the very next day. My mother didn't want them in her business. She would have cussed them out if I had told her that they were asking me all this stuff.

Thank God, we moved away from those stupid old ladies to our own house.

Even though Herbert got on my nerves, he was a really good brother. He did not let anybody bother me. One time, a boy called me a really bad name because I would not talk to him, and Herbert banged him in his face—fast! While the boy was trying to pick himself up from the ground, I yelled, "That's what you get for messing with me. That's why my brother beat your tail!" Julia would have been so proud of him.

On second thought, how did Herbert find out about this incident, and how did he get there so fast? He always thought that he was Superman, and maybe he was, especially since Julia said that he could beat anybody in the world. *Well, whatever.* He found out from somewhere, and that was the last time anybody in my neighborhood, especially a boy, ever called me anything. He was even ready to bang a girl in the face when she tried to fight me because she said that my mouth was too big. I wish he had banged her. She was so ugly. One bang in the mouth would have kept her in her place. Well, I am so glad that Herbert beat that boy up, because if he hadn't, Julia would have beaten Herbert's butt. She used to tell him, "If you can't beat 'em with your fist, get a bat and beat the sh—— out of them!" Oops, that's a bad word and Julia said that we had better not say bad words or she would beat the piss or sh—— out of us.

Well, anyway, when we were growing up, my brother Herbert and I were absolutely afraid of the wrath of our mother, Julia. We knew that if we did anything wrong, no matter how small, the beat down would be brutal. The welts would sting for hours, with little or no relief for a day or two. This single mother was no one to play with. If she said, "In the house by seven o'clock," one second after seven o'clock was too late. In the summer months when my brother was a teenager, she would let him stay out until nine o'clock, and I remember hearing his running footsteps as he ran to get not just to our house, but in the house, before the last church bell rang.

One time, Herbert "found" a dime on the dining room table, and he spent it. Little did he know that the dime belonged to Julia. She had left it on the table for one of us to purchase bread from the corner store. When she returned with the additional fifteen cents needed to buy a loaf of bread and saw that the dime was not there, she became flaming mad. She made Herbert close his hand to make a fist so that she could "crack" his knuckles with a ruler, and she beat his knuckles for what seemed like an hour. As she beat, she drilled, "Don't you ever take anything that does not belong to you." One thing I can say about Herbert is that while we were growing up, he did not take any more dimes from tables in our house or anybody else's house.

Yeah, Julia was rough and tough, but she loved us. She worked two jobs to take care of us, and when she could, she would buy us anything that we wanted. Back then, we only wanted skates, bikes, dolls, toy guns, and money to spend on our way to school. One time, when it snowed so badly that school was out for about a week, Julia made us put on three layers of clothes so that we could play in the snow. When our toes froze and we were forced to go inside, she had hot chocolate waiting for us while she dried our clothing on the radiators, so that once we got warm, we could go right back out to play in the snow. When everybody else's mother would not let them come back out, Julia always said, "I don't care where you go!" Right on, Julia!

Julia did have one obsessive-compulsive problem that made Herbert and me steaming mad. However, she never knew that we were mad, because if we had shown any expressions that looked like disrespect, the consequences would have been severe. Julia wanted her house to be clean at all times. She never cleaned it; we had to. At seven years old, I washed dishes, fixed meals, washed clothes, ironed—you name it, she taught me how to do it! Herbert had to take out the trash, walk the dog, clean up after the dog, and watch me. Here we go again. Oh, God, I hated it when he had to watch me. He was like a hawk, watching every little step I took. While Julia worked, Herbert had to make sure that both of us completed our homework before going outside, and we had to be back in the house by seven o'clock. At 7:05 on the dot, Julia called to make sure that we were in the house—not coming into the house, but in the house.

Well, Julia did have another little obsessive-compulsive problem. She was a fashion statement all by herself. Every hair was in place, skirts and blouses were starched and ironed, and shoes matched the outfits. Her hair was well-groomed, and she wore lots of make-up. Men always told me that my mother was "very attractive," and she really was—and still is. Julia was in full control of her world. She could cuss like a sailor, drink scotch with the best of them, and smoke a pack or two of Salem cigarettes every day. Back then, we could run to the corner store and buy cigarettes for her out of these machines that had knobs we had to pull to dispense the cigarettes.

Oops, I forgot. Julia had another obsessive-compulsive problem. Herbert and I had to go to church every single Sunday. She would straighten my hair with a hot straightening comb every Sunday morning, making my grandfather so mad. He used to tell her that all she was doing was taking my hair out. She did not care what he said, but I did. As soon as he came into the house, I would start crying because I was tender-headed (that's what they called it back then). Well, anyway, my grandfather hated it when we cried. He would hug me when Julia finished my hair and tell me not to cry. It didn't matter, because I still got my hair straightened every Sunday, and every Sunday, we went to church. Some Sundays, we would sneak over to Uncle Sammy's house and not go to church. We spent our church money on candy. Herbert and I both promised not to tell Julia. Boy oh boy, if Julia had known, she would have killed us. (At least, that's what she said when she was mad and getting ready to beat us.)

One time, I prayed and asked God to strike her hand so that she wouldn't beat me. Even though she laughed about my prayer later that day, I still got the beating. Back then, I would get a beating just for being sassy to the adults in the neighborhood. I never knew that they could even hear me, because I whispered. Well, those were the good ol' days. Everybody watched everybody's children. You could not do anything because somebody's mother was always watching. They always told Julia everything that Herbert and I did. If I so much as got off the steps, they told. Even though Herbert kept getting into fights, it was not their business. Too bad Julia didn't beat them; she sure did beat us enough.

I don't know what was worse, getting a beating or getting "punished," which meant staying in our rooms for one month. We could not even come out for meals. Julia would make a bag lunch for us and bring it to our room. For Herbert, sometimes the bag lunch was bread and water. She would say, "You want to know what jail is like? Well, here is your bread and water—just what they serve in jail!"

Before she left for work, she dared the one that was punished to come out of the room. Guess what? We did not come out unless we had to go to the bathroom. We were too scared. Usually, only one of us was punished at a time. The one not punished was responsible for telling Julia what the other one did. So if Herbert was punished, I had to make sure that he stayed in the room. The worst part was that when he was punished, I was not allowed outside. If I was punished, he didn't have to stay in the house, but he had to stay close enough to watch me.

Take a deep breath and journey with me as I try to describe Julia's current world through a conversation with her:

"Julia, how did you, a woman who was so in control of your life, lose that control so fast? It is just not fair. You have to get it together and just come back. You are not the same person. Now you need someone to watch you twenty-four seven. You are not the Julia who walked tall in high heeled-shoes, and wore starched skirts, matching blouses, and dark red lipstick. There was not a hair out of place and your long black ponytail was perfectly beautiful. The ponytail was your signature for years, and no one wore Chinese bangs the way you did.

"I know that you are somewhere inside that brain. Just get it together, and come back! Did I tell you that one of your cousins passed away? Remember, you used to call me when somebody in our family passed or was in the hospital. I need to tell you stuff, but you just sit there and stare at me or respond by saying something that has absolutely nothing to do with what I am telling you. I'll tell you one thing: if there is a cure for this disease, I will find it. You will come back. I am not going to let some stupid disease take my mother away from me. I mean that. By the way, I talked to Ronaldo yesterday and he told me to tell you that he loves you! I know that you haven't seen him for the past eleven years. Remember when I took you to see him?"

It seemed that I was having this conversation with myself, because Julia started asking questions about her mother, my grandmother who had passed away several years ago.

"Holley, did you see Mother today?" Julia asked in the middle of our conversation.

"No, Julia, I did not see her today, but do you remember when I took you to see Ronaldo?"

"Yeah, I saw Ronaldo just now. He is still in school."

"Julia, do you want a cup of coffee?"

"Yeah, I want coffee."

At least I have learned that if I want to bring Julia into a conversation that has an ounce of meaning to her, I have to offer something that she recognizes and loves—**coffee.**

CHAPTER 2
A Crash Course

One day, our world started crashing down around us. My brother kept getting into trouble, mainly fighting. I had to go to the city jail at least once a year to bail him out. Then we moved from place to place. I remember moving ten times in ten years. Our gas and electric was off more than it was on. Julia got married to a crazy man who wanted to fight her all the time, and my brother tried to kill him. If my cousin, Lawrence, had not been there, Herbert would have killed my mother's husband. There were times when we had to eat grits for breakfast, lunch, and dinner. And one time, Julia did not have money to buy us anything for Christmas, and she cried all day and all week.

Then her brother died, and that set her back badly. He used to call her once a week, and they would laugh on the phone. Since he was in the army and stationed in a different time zone from ours, this meant that he would be calling my mother at 4:00 a.m., or, when he was stationed in Germany, sometime after midnight. I remember that after one New Year's Day, my mother went to work and told her co-workers that she had washed clothes all day on New Year's Day.

Alarmed, her co-workers chided, "Girl, don't you know better than that? You wash away somebody in your family when you wash on New Year's Day!"

Right after that, she got the dreaded phone call that her brother Herman had died in a car crash. She was devastated. She loved Uncle Herman so much. My grandparents lost their only son, and my mother lost her only brother. Julia tried to understand how God could have let such a thing happen to her.

Julia continued to act like the "I'm in control woman," but things really did get worse, and losing her one and only brother was just the beginning. Religion became her saving grace. It became a way to "soothe her soul," as she said. She made sure that Herbert and I were baptized, and that we said our prayers before every meal and before we went to bed, even if she wasn't at home. One year, we joined a Baptist church, and the very next year, we were Jehovah's Witnesses. Back then, everybody in our community celebrated Children's Day, and Julia would take her last dime to make sure that we looked really great on that Sunday. I had Shirley Temple curls and Herbert had to put on a suit and tie. We really looked good. Julia did not always go to church with us, but she made us go anyway.

PAUSE for Another Conversation with Julia

"Julia, don't you even remember when Herbert and I got baptized? You were there, remember? It was at the church across the street from Uncle Sammy's house. I had on a white gown, and so did Herbert. Remember when the pastor and his wife drove us home and you tried to pay them, but they would not take your money? You have to remember that. You were crying because you were so happy that we were getting baptized, and you came in the back to help us put our clothes back on. Just say that you remember! Just say it! Nobody forgets something as special as that."

Julia just sat and stared into space. There was no expression on her face. She looked at me and I looked at her. She didn't even know where we were.

> *Was anybody listening to my cries; as I brushed back the hair from her eyes?*
>
> *Does anyone know about this nightmare, or does anyone really care?*

Is this a battle that you go alone? A journey into the un-
known—
Where dreams die and children cry!

The weddings missed, and grandchildren not kissed.
The sleepless nights and times when nothing goes right!

Blank stares, burdens to bear, and many prayers!
No time for despair … just know that God cares!

I was determined to make Julia recognize us in this picture:

"Julia, who are the two children in this picture? There is absolutely no way that you do not know that this is Herbert and me! What is wrong with you? You are making me cry! Open your eyes, and just look at the picture. That's me on the right and that's Herbert on the left! We both were dressed in white. Julia, remember these words from one of your favorite songs: 'On a hill far away stood an old rugged Cross.' Then you can remember when this picture was taken. You have to remember! This is a picture of your children, Peanut and Herbert. There is just no reason that you cannot remember when we were young. Nobody forgets their own children. And stop calling me Holley! My name is Peanut! That's what you used to call me!"

CHAPTER 3
A Glimmer of Hope

Julia found happiness again (for one hot minute) with her new husband and her new family of two more children. It was like starting all over again!

Herbert hated Julia's new life, and his encounters with prison life increased. His encounters with substance abuse started and never stopped. We tolerated her new husband, but we worried because he was always sitting around while she worked like a dog. It was kind of hard on her, trying to work and take care of two new children and a husband. Well, I was sixteen years old when she started her new family, so I was planning on getting married myself and moving out of her house, especially to get away from her new husband. The glimmer of hope did not last long. Julia's life did not get easier after she got married; it became more complicated. She found out that she had lupus, a disease that forced her to retire from a job that she had held for years without ever missing a day. She worked when no one else worked. When I think about it, retiring was probably a good thing for Julia.

Then my grandfather passed away, and that was one of the most devastating blows in our family. He was the center of our lives. He tried to take care of his grandchildren, his adult children, and even other people and their children. He made our world go around and around, and it stopped turning when he died. I hate that word "died." Even though Julia didn't say it, she missed him more than anyone would ever know. I am even having a hard time writing this, because my grandfather, Daniel Ross, was the center of our hearts. Julia told us hundreds of stories about her father and how much she loved him. She called him "Daddy." Every Christmas, he came to our house or apartment and picked us up to take us to his house for dinner. That was the highlight of our Christmas. Many times, Julia could not afford to buy us anything, but we didn't care. Going to my grandfather's house was enough for us. He and my grandmother had so much food, and many people came to their house for dinner. Julia loved it; we were always the last ones to go home. Yes, my grandfather had to take us back home. Then he went home to be with God, and this was the end of phase two of Julia's attempt to make sense out of a life that was rapidly wearing her down.

PAUSE for another attempt to have a conversation with Julia in her current condition!

Every time I drive Julia anywhere, she blurts out, "Daddy asked me if I wanted to learn how to drive, and I told him, 'No, Daddy. I just want to drink.' Daddy would just burst out laughing and say, 'Well, baby, I guess you won't ever drive.'" Julia then starts laughing.

A few minutes later, Julia again blurts out, "Daddy asked me if I wanted to learn how to drive, and I told him, 'No, Daddy. I just want to drink.' Daddy would burst out laughing and say, 'Well, baby, I guess you won't ever drive.'"

The only way to end this banter is to get Julia something to eat or to turn on the radio. Every now and then, you can tell from the look in her eyes that she recognizes an artist like Sam Cooke or Brook Benton or James Brown on the radio, and the conversation about her father ends—until she gets into my car the next time. This was an early sign that Julia was beginning to slip into a world that included no one else, a world that only her eyes could see.

Julia's Dad! A love missed!

CHAPTER 4
Julia, the Best Grandmother Ever

Julia became the babysitter for my two youngest children, and oh my God, they loved her. She let them do anything and everything. She let them buy candy with her food stamps, and she bought five Big Wheels during one visit to a Goodwill Store so that their friends could have something to ride. She scrambled them a dozen of eggs, a pack of bacon, and loads of pancakes each morning for their breakfast. If my younger brother and sister wanted to eat, they had to get up before my girls fed the neighborhood children.

Once, my girls asked if they could spend the summer with Julia, and my husband and I both said, "Absolutely not," because we knew that they would get away with doing anything they wanted to. Finally, we gave in and allowed them to spend two nights with Julia. I was ready to pick them up one hour after leaving them, because Julia let them go outside in the rain to take their baths. Oh, My God, did their father have a hissy fit. He swore that they would never go back to Julia's house again, but he was no match for Julia.

When we arrived to pick them up after work, Julia could not find them, and she thought it was funny. When we finally found them, they looked as if they had been playing in mud and dirt all day, but they were the happiest two little girls. They cried when their father threatened not to let them go back the next day. But who else was going to watch them? Julia had ruined them and there was no turning back. They loved her unconditionally. They learned to cuss like sailors, and they were even hoping that Julia would let them smoke cigarettes. Thank God, they finally went to school all day, because there is absolutely no telling what Julia would have let them do. Just ask them and they will tell you to this day that Julia was the best grandmother in the whole wide world.

And then one day, Julia did not recognize them at all. Something had taken Julia away from them … something that is hard to describe.

"Julia, do you know these two girls in this picture?"

"No, but you do?"

"Who are these two girls, Julia?"

"They must be two little girls!"

"Julia, these two little girls are your granddaughters."

"That's good!"

Oh, My God! I thought. She does not even recognize Kera and Taryn. She does not even recognize any of her grandchildren!

So, what happened? Maybe she had a nervous breakdown. Well, if that's the case, she can recover from that. Maybe it's because she abruptly stopped drinking. She stopped cold turkey on the day Aunt Peale passed. She loved Aunt Peale, and she depended on her for advice. I cannot figure this out.

"So, Julia, go to sleep, and when you wake up, all of this will be over. You will come back and you will remember your grandchildren!"

We love you, Granny!

CHAPTER 5
In the Midst of It All

Then Julia's husband became sick, and he never recovered. She was angry with him for reasons that I cannot explain. Was it because he got sick? Was she just depressed? She didn't even want to go to see him while he was hospitalized. You could tell that she was sad about his death, but she kept a stiff upper lip. I wonder if she cried while she was alone in her room. I never saw her grieve over him, but I did see a change in Julia.

She began "cussing" more. The house that she rented began to look even more like a junk yard, with antiques, more furniture in the smallest rooms, clutter everywhere, clothes and linen piled high from the floor to the ceiling, and plants everywhere—most dead or dying.

One day, Julia lost the keys to her house and climbed up a ladder to the second floor of her row house to try to get in. She fell and broke her leg in several places. She was hospitalized, and pins were inserted into her leg to help the bones heal. For reasons unknown to any of us, Julia left the hospital without being discharged. After several weeks, the leg began to swell, and it was showing signs of severe infection. We had to make her return to the hospital so that they could remove the pins, especially since she'd told the doctors that she was not staying "in no f—— hospital!"

CHAPTER 6
A Fifty-Nine-Year Prison Sentence

My youngest brother and Julia's baby, Ronaldo, was a four-time offender. They finally sent him away for fifty-nine years. Ronaldo was the love of Julia's life. She loved him. She worshipped the ground that he walked on. When he was sentenced, she acted like she didn't care, but she did. I never saw her cry about it, and, again, she kept a stiff upper lip and would say things like, "A hard head makes a soft ass!"

Ronaldo was in prison for three years before she went to see him, and by that time, she was beginning to show severe signs of dementia. As soon as she saw him, she started telling him how she was going to get him out of there. She assured him over and over again that she knew "the man" and that she would give "the man" her whole check to get him out of jail. This was Julia's way of trying to show that she was still in control.

Today, Julia rarely asks about Ronaldo. Occasionally, out of the blue, she asks, "Has anybody seen Ronaldo today? I guess he is okay. He told me that he was coming over today." One time, Julia said, "Has anybody seen Ronaldo today? I guess he's okay. He gave me this money (holding a nickel in her hand) and told me that I could have it."

When she said that, I became angry and began to lose it. "Julia, you know that Ronaldo did not give you that nickel, so why don't you just stop it. Stop it, Julia! I don't know how to help you! I don't know what to do! Every time I look at you, I cry! There are times when you act like you are normal, and then the very next moment, you act like you are in another world. That's okay. You are going to a doctor tomorrow to get some medicine whether you want to or not! Whether you want to or not and I mean it!"

The tears would not stop rolling down my face.

PAUSE: A Conversation with Julia

"Julia, maybe God doesn't want you to remember. Maybe he is making it easier for you to forget the pains in your life. Occasionally you talk about Nanny. You always tell me about your father asking you if you wanted to learn how to drive. Once in a while, you ask about Herbert, and once in a while you ask, "Has anybody seen Pretty today?" I sometimes remind you that Rock, your husband, is deceased. Sometimes, I just say that I have not seen him in a while. When you ask if I have seen Nanny, I sometimes tell you that I have. Often, I have to hop into your world just to help you make sense of your new world. I am sorry for what I said yesterday, but I could not help myself. At least you have some new medications. The doctor thinks that you may have Alzheimer's disease, and he advised me to consider placing you in a nursing home. Well, that won't happen! Let him put his mother into a nursing home.

"Come on! Let's go to Repeat Performance and buy some clothes. I think that the Bag Sale is today and you can put a lot of clothes in a bag for ten dollars. Then, we are going to Boston Market to eat lunch. You like their chicken and mashed potatoes. You'll be okay. You will get better. I just know it. So, don't worry! Did you hear me, Julia? Did you hear me?

Silence.

CHAPTER 8
Early Signs

Inside her house, where anybody and everybody took up residence, you could find stacks and stacks of linen and clothes piled up against the walls in her bedroom, unfilled prescriptions, and no food.

Twice more, she fell and broke her leg (at least that's what she said happened), and each time, she left the hospital without being discharged. Neighbors reported that Julia visited dumpsters daily and carted away all kinds of stuff, even food that had been thrown away by others. Friends and family members called when they saw Julia walking late at night with shopping carts filled with items that she had gotten from the dumpsters. She often walked from West Baltimore to East Baltimore, even in inclement weather. She had an undying love for her mother, and she just had to see her as often as possible, even daily, when possible. Several times, she walked twenty miles from Pikesville in Baltimore County to West Baltimore Street in Baltimore City just to see her mother. Trying to find Julia during the many times that she disappeared was scary, but not always too difficult because she stopped to talk to people and to ask for directions along the way. She knew where she wanted to go, but she occasionally got lost. She was on a mission and it didn't matter how she got there.

Once she was missing for about four or five hours, and I was mortified. However, I know that the God I serve is always watching over Julia. He has always known her heart. On that night, thanks to

God, Julia had traveled to Mondawmin Mall, and someone from her old neighborhood recognized her and found a way to get in touch with me. That was truly a blessed day. When I found Julia, she was not hurt at all. She smiled when she saw me and said, "Holley, I am so glad you came. I was looking for you." It was on this day that I realized that God was watching over Julia, and that no one could or would ever harm her again. God knew her heart, and He used her heart to guide her safely through paths unknown to us!

PAUSE: A Conversation with Julia

"Julia, I am so sorry that you are suffering from such a very debilitating disease. I believe that God is helping you not to remember so many blows in life that just pulled you down. We have not always seen eye to eye, but I remember the great things that you did as a mother. I remember you sitting up all night because Herbert and I were both sick at the same time. I remember you making us eat hot soup whenever we were sick because you felt that it would make us feel better. I remember the time that you dared Herbert to hit me after I called him a name, and I remember the times that you told everyone that you met that I was your baby. I remember when Pretty was born and you said that she was so ugly, and because of that you named her Pretty. She really did get to be pretty as she got older. I remember when Ronaldo was born and his legs were long and crooked, and his eyes would cross. I remember the many tears that you shed when you could not buy me a pair of skates for Christmas; I remember when your brother died; I remember when your father passed; I remember the times when…"

Julia, do you remember?

CHAPTER 7
Gone Are the Days

As Julia's control began to dwindle away, anybody and everybody took up residence in her house. She helped to raise two grandchildren and other people's children. Then homeless adults moved in "until they got on their feet," but that never happened. As the checks went missing each month, the gas and electric was turned off. Often there was no food. Each month for three years, my grandmother called to tell me that somebody had stolen one of Julia's checks. Then Julia would call each month to say that she had "lost" one of her checks. Then the federal government stopped sending her checks because her address was changed several times by some unknown person, and the signatures on the checks did not match. One or two of her checks were returned to them and stamped "Addressee Unknown." There was even a young lady who managed to get an ID card in Julia's name with Julia's social security number, but it did not have Julia's picture on the front of the ID. The manager of the check cashing establishment was not able to explain how that happened.

The entire situation was bizarre. On the same day that Julia received and cashed her retirement or social security checks, at least half or all of her money was stolen. Some went to pay a loan shark who allowed Julia and my grandmother to borrow money and pay it back on "check day." Then, according to "family members," Julia lost the rest of the money. No one will ever know where or how

Julia lost her money, but it was gone. Little did the thieves know that their behavior would someday bring Julia down!

Then Julia moved back to her old neighborhood, and things got even worse. At least six people moved in with her, and none of them paid rent, bought food, or helped with anything else. Her gas and electric were turned off again, and there were many times that she did not even have food to eat. Upon my arrival at a local hospital's emergency room where Julia had gone one day because she was sick, hospital staff informed me that Julia had crawled across a busy street that was covered with ice on her hands and knees trying to get to the emergency room, because she was just that ill. They even noted that she had been there before, but they were not sure if she had taken her medicine the first time. On that cold icy day, she wore only plastic thong shoes (no socks), a slip, and a trench coat.

Once they diagnosed her condition, the physician prescribed some antibiotics for her, and that was the day that I stepped in and went ballistic: "First of all, why are you just writing her a prescription?" I asked the ignorant doctor. "If her behavior is so bizarre and you have no evidence that she got the first prescription filled, why would you send her back home without first treating her here?"

That was the stupidest—or most negligent—hospital in the world. I wanted to say to them, "Do not let the Julia in me come out, because if it does, it will not be pretty!" I held my tongue after that. Well, anyway, they did give her an antibiotic intravenously while I watched, and in a couple of days, she was much better.

I remember returning to see Julia the next day after her visit to the emergency room to find that she had not eaten all day because there was no food in the house, even though my adult sister lived there, along with a young lady and her small son, a man who lived in the basement with his sons, and two cousins. Once, a deceased Caucasian female had been found on the living room sofa. The house had no electricity and was in a state of extreme disrepair. If I brought Julia hot food from a restaurant, I had to sit with her until she ate every drop, so that her non-paying tenants would not beg and consume her first meal for that day.

Stepping in was not easy. One of the local hospitals admitted Julia upon my request for an observation because of her bizarre behavior and because they felt that she just was not capable of taking care of herself. Even though they initially advised that she be transferred to a long-term care facility, I chose not to transfer her to one. My grandmother allowed Julia to stay with her for a while, until it became too much for her to handle. Every day, my grandmother called to tell me about Julia's "strange" behavior. Once, my grandmother called and told me that she could not take it anymore, because Julia kept saying the same thing over and over again, and she was hiding food under her mattress, in the closet, and in her dresser drawers. I then arranged for her to move into a different community with her own apartment, fully furnished and with plenty of food. The predators moved in and stayed until I allowed the lease to expire.

As her condition worsened, it became a matter of urgency, and I made an effort to save her from herself and her predators (family and friends). She was admitted to a long-term care facility. Initially, this was a great decision because Julia gained more than fifty pounds, and she really did look great. At one point, a smidgen of the old Julia emerged. She was snappy and bossy and no one, absolutely no one, was in charge of Julia. I escorted Julia, her new friends, and her roommate to play bingo on Thursdays, and I took her shopping every week.

Ms. Julia's journey does not end here! The journey has a new beginning!

CHAPTER 9
Progress

So far, Julia's progress has been measured by the length of time that it has taken for her to move from one stage of Alzheimer's disease to the next stage. At the beginning of Julia's journey, her behaviors were described as bizarre. The wandering, the confusion, the dumpster visits, and other behaviors simply defined the paths that Julia was taking. I am not sure if this is the path that all patients with Alzheimer's disease follow. I had a great-uncle who had Alzheimer's disease, and he began to sit for long periods of time, just staring into space. Julia began sitting and staring into space at the onset of the disease, and the same was happening eight years after her first episode of bizarre behaviors (wandering, visiting dumpsters).

When she started walking long distances to find her mother, I began to realize that she needed intensive care and could not adequately take care of herself. She could dress herself if her clothes were selected and presented to her. She could feed herself once the food was placed in front of her. She was even taking care of bodily functions with some assistance (e.g., cleaning, sanitizing her hands).

Then incontinence set in, and Ms. Julia needed assistance with changing her clothes. At times, she informs us when she feels the need to urinate or make a bowel movement. Then there are days when she just does not remember to alert us, and it just happens.

Eight years into the disease, Ms. Julia needed around-the-clock care that included helping her to walk or exercise, assisting her with eating, and especially, assisting with her bathroom needs that could include actually sitting her on the commode. Is this stage easier? No, because emotionally it drains your very soul to see someone that you dearly love in this condition.

On February 3, 2011, Ms. Julia had what looked very much like a stroke or a seizure. Both were ruled out; however, during the seizure-like episode, she let out a loud scream, her eyes rolled back in her head, her arms went limp, and she did not respond for several minutes. When the ambulance arrived, her blood pressure was 80/30, and her pulse was weak. The diagnosis did not confirm a seizure. She was treated for an unspecified infection. She complained of pains in her stomach and back, but the attending physicians and nurses dismissed the pain as being related to confusion. I insisted that she did have pain. On previous occasions, when she'd been under my care, she had complained of pain but responded to pain medication (ibuprofen). After ingesting the pain meds, Julia would bounce back and not complain of pain again until it returned. Often the abdominal pain was related to not being able to have a bowel movement; when this was the case, I would give her a stool softener. It worked like magic and the pain went away.

After the episode of what appeared to be a stroke or a seizure, Julia had a major setback and did not take the initiative to move from one place to another or even walk around the house anymore. Prior to the "seizure," she would let me know when she wanted something to eat, but then I have to just fix the food, place it in front of her, and assist her with eating it. The staring was not encouraging, because she would stare in the same direction for hours if I let her. I simply called her name to get her attention, but then there were times when she did not even respond to this. The only option I had was to help her to stand up and then support her while walking with her around the house or up and down our street.

Along with the staring, Ms. Julia began to lean forward and would place her head on her knees as if she was curling up her body. While she was sleeping, her legs would be bent at the knees with her heels almost touching her buttocks. Her movement became rigid, and attempts to dress and undress her became very difficult, because her arms stiffened, and she would grab her clothing to stop you from attending to her. She loved to just stay in bed and would not even make an attempt to get up on her own. She had to be lifted from her bed and placed in an upright position to get her moving. She would take only one step at a time when tugged.

After the "seizure," Julia stopped communicating with everyone. Now that was truly a big change. Occasionally, she would respond with one or two words when asked a question. Then there were times when she did not respond at all. I was concerned about whether or not I could get Ms. Julia going again. To do so would definitely require lots of work. Engaging her worked in the past, and this was the only possible way to get her back to being Ms. Julia again. My action plan included talking to her throughout the day and waiting for responses. I knew that I would need to get her up from her chair and/or bed and help her walk around the house. Taking her to the mall where lots of people hung out worked to stimulate her brain. Listening to music prompted her to pat her feet and even move her head from side to side. She also loved to watch cartoons; I am not sure why.

Am I considering a long term care facility? No. I feel that I can pretty much take care of her with some assistance from my immediate family. The most difficult task was trying to get Ms. Julia from my house and into my truck for doctors' appointments, or for trips to do grocery shopping.

And the progress begins!

Immediately after being released from a second hospital (three emergency visits, two admissions, a colonoscopy, CT scans, x-rays, blood work, and antibiotic infusions), Ms. Julia was discharged, and the discharge instructions were void of any reference to the "seizure" (if it was a seizure). Who knows? Since no one knew what was wrong with Julia, it made me mad! I was determined to find a way to bring Ms. Julia back.

First, I prayed and prayed and prayed. I just was not ready to let Ms. Julia go. The hospital social worker referred Ms. Julia for home health care, and this included a visiting nurse and a physical therapist. I requested a hospital bed and she got one.

They requested a new wheelchair, and she got one. The visiting nurse and the physical therapist were outstanding. First of all, they listened to my experiences with Ms. Julia. She could not tell them about her history, or how she was feeling, so they asked me and *they listened.*

Then, since no one was able to definitively diagnose the "seizure-like episode" that set her back, I contacted a rheumatologist to have someone, at least one professional, look at her lupus. In the eight years that I have been taking care of Ms. Julia, and even after I told every single physician (both hospital and primary care physicians) that she had lupus and was first diagnosed approximately forty years ago, they all ignored that and continued to treat her "Alzheimer's disease/dementia" primarily with prescription drugs to manage her behaviors. I initiated a daily regimen of vitamins, exercise, and routines that included scheduled meals, a time to watch cartoons (that she enjoys), trips to the mall, shopping at consignment shops (thrift stores), and times to listen to the radio; occasionally she recognized a song and responded with head movements and feet patting.

Well, the rheumatologist examined her from head to toe. Her primary care physician barely touched her. The rheumatologist ordered a battery of tests. At one point, I thought she would not have any blood left in her body (just kidding), but he was thorough and did not want to leave any stone unturned. He did not prescribe any medications following the initial visit, because he wanted to make sure that if she did have lupus, he could begin treating her for it.

Well, on the second visit, he examined her again from head to toe, confirmed a diagnosis of lupus, and referred her to a neurologist to determine why she had the "seizure-like episodes." He then prescribed a medication for the lupus. This occurred after he was 100 percent sure that she had lupus. Within one week, Ms. Julia was making her way back! A sure sign that she was back was when she started cursing! Oh, joy! Those curse words were music to my ears. Then she started singing and engaging in conversations with others. She began to initiate conversations and even began to tell us that she was hungry. Oh, joy!

The visit to the neurologist was just as rewarding. He was superb as well. He talked to Ms. Julia, and he touched her by examining her reflexes, her arm and leg movements, and her sucking reflexes. When he stuck her with a pin, she hit him. He was not offended at all, and as a matter of fact, he laughed. I tried not to laugh, but after seeing him laugh, I began laughing and crying. Oh, joy! Before leaving his office, I was quite sure that the "seizure-like episode" was a transient ischemic attack, because the neurologist was well versed on the topic, and he was not guessing like some doctors do.

If you, as the reader, get nothing else out of my experiences with Ms. Julia, please remember that finding the best doctors work. Finding good doctors was my constant prayer, and I did not let anything stand in the way of that. Sure, some doctors may get offended when you ask them questions or press for answers; but so be it!

So, what else works for Ms. Julia?

1. Keeping Julia engaged works for Ms. Julia. Although nothing that I have done has helped her to remember the names of various close family members, keeping her engaged has helped to:

    *   Make her feel like my home is definitely her home. She has no problem walking around the house, folding clothes, getting a cup of water, looking out the window, stepping outside the front door and coming back inside (especially when she realizes that it is too cold), and sitting in her favorite seat in the kitchen to eat her meals.
    *   Lessen incidents of anxiety, especially since she sees the same faces daily.

Some of the ways that I keep Ms. Julia engaged include:

*   Sitting with her to eat dinner, to watch television, and to listen to religious broadcasts. In addition, we laugh and sing with her.
*   Arranging for the great-grandchild that she loves to visit weekly. We can tell that he makes her happy because of her facial expressions. She gets

extraordinarily happy when she sees him, and she will not take her eyes off of him; when he moves, she moves.

- Taking her for a ride in the truck each day. She watches out the windows and occasionally will say something about the people that she sees. For example, it seems that she likes to count people, and she will blurt out, "There goes three ladies," or "Look at that fat man!"
- Watching country music videos with her. Why country videos, I do not know! Whatever the reason, she likes them and will even pat one foot to the music.
- Dancing. She likes it when someone dances. To keep her happy and engaged, I use dancing as a form of exercise for myself. Ms. Julia's face lights up each time I dance in front of her. Occasionally, she will say, "You are doing it!"
- Placing snacks in front of her—one piece at a time. She reaches for any snacks that are in front of her, and she even waits for the next piece.
- Prompting her to argue with us. For example, if my husband says something about my sister, Julia will curse like a sailor. This tends to get her pumped up and very engaged. If nothing else, she has not forgotten how to curse, and she does it extremely well.

2. Routines work for Ms. Julia. Some of these routines are a little similar to activities that engage Ms. Julia. They include:
    - Beginning her mornings with bathroom activities that include assisting with toiletry needs, washing her face and/or assisting her with washing her own face, rinsing her mouth, and washing her hands
    - Saving her favorite seat at the kitchen table just for her. When she sees me place napkins on the table,

she responds by going right to her favorite seat, where she sits anticipating a meal until she gets a meal.

- Sitting with her to watch game shows and cartoons. I think she likes the bright colors and the noises of these shows. On the flip side of this, when I am watching the news, she begins to just stare into space.
- Letting her get into the car on the same side, where she is familiar with the support bars that she uses to lift herself into the car.
- Getting her ready for bed at approximately the same time nightly. This is almost effortless, except for undressing her, which tends to present some challenges. She just does not like having anyone undress her. Once she is settled into the bed, she stays there.
- Making sure that her three-year-old great-grandson visits her weekly. She recognizes him immediately (not his name, but that he is her "baby"). She even tries to chase him around the house, but catching this little whippersnapper is not easy for Julia.
- Keeping her shoes and socks in the same location so that she can easily find them and put them on. She has not forgotten how to put on her socks and shoes.
- Leaving a cup on the table where she sits for most meals. At least three or four times daily, she will use the cup to get drinking water. This task amazes us, because this is the only time that she makes an effort on her own to satisfy a need (thirst).
- Always putting the towels that she likes to fold in the same place for her to find and fold.

The routines work, but changing a routine also works. I think it stimulates her brain. For example, if I move her favorite chair, she gets a little anxious and will actually move her chair right back to where she wants to sit.

Once, when she fractured her right arm because she put on slippery shoes and would not allow anyone to take them off, she was forced to use her left arm. Julia's ability to engage in conversations with others improved significantly. She called me by my name for the first time in ten years, asked about the time, and when asked where she lived, she stated (without hesitation), "In Baltimore." We were floored.

A How-to List for Ms. Julia

How to Get Ms. Julia Undressed

Getting Ms. Julia undressed is not easy, because she stiffens her arms and will not let you take off her clothes. It is as if she is protecting her privacy. So, to make it easier, I begin by talking to her to take her mind off what I am doing. Then with the utmost speed, I take each arm out first. While she is still trying to understand what I am talking about, I lift her clothing over her head. Usually, I can pull everything over her head at the same time.

To change her (disposable) underwear, I usually just tear each side and then pull it off.

Getting her shoes off is a little easier if you have lightning speed. I just take them off really fast before she even realizes what I am doing. I make sure that she is sitting when I do this!

How to Get Julia Dressed

Getting Ms. Julia to put on her clothes is not easy, because you have to guide each arm into the clothing quickly, one arm at a time. Then, you must continue to talk to her while dressing her so that she does not think that you are trying to take off her clothes.

Getting her shoes on is a piece of cake. I just put the shoes in front of her and she will walk toward them and will actually put her feet into the shoes.

How to Negotiate the Use of the Bathroom

Okay! Here we go! At one time, Ms. Julia would just walk into the bathroom, on her own, when she was told to get ready to take a bath. At that time, I only had to help her get into the tub and then help her to sit down.

Now, the process is quite different. First, to get her into the bathroom, I have to hold her arms in front of her while I stand behind her, guiding her into the bathroom. Once inside the bathroom, I begin with the undressing. Once that is over, I get her into the tub by lifting one of her feet into the tub while she holds onto my neck.

Then I put the second foot into the tub and hold her steady while lowering her onto the seat.

Getting her out of the tub is a bit different. I gently turn her toward me, and then I lift one leg at a time and place them over the side of the tub. Then, I put my arms under her arms, and I gently lift her from the tub seat.

The Toilet Is Quite Different

At one time, Ms. Julia would just sit on the toilet as soon as she entered the bathroom. Now, you have to talk her through it, while at the same time guiding her to the toilet—back first. Then, while telling her to sit, I have to gently move her feet (with my feet) to get her in position to sit down. Sometimes, I have to actually lift her up with my hands under her legs (to slightly bend them for sitting). Once she is seated, I turn on the water, her brain responds, and she urinates.

I can usually tell when she needs to make a bowel movement, because she gets fidgety. When this happens, I just take her to the bathroom, and 99 percent of the time, she has to and does make a bowel movement.

The most important part of the entire bathroom process is cleaning her afterward. I have my equipment ready to go. I fill the sink with very warm water, and I add an antibacterial solution and a mild soap to the water. I use wet wipes because they are more sanitary; washcloths hold germs. I wipe once with a wipe and then toss it in the trash. I continue to use more wipes until I am absolutely sure that she is clean.

Sometimes, I use an antibacterial spray solution, and I then spray the solution all over her private areas. Again, I use wet wipes to wipe the solution off. Once I am absolutely sure that she is clean (and this may mean using a lot of wipes), I pat her dry and put on a protective cream; and I then I put on clean disposable underwear. Look for protective creams and antimicrobial cleansers to decrease bacteria, and a skin protection paste to prevent rashes.

Once this entire process is completed, I thoroughly sanitize the bathroom in preparation for the next time. I keep the bathroom fully stocked with all the things needed for Ms. Julia. I even keep plastic bags (grocery bags will do) under the sink to make it easier to dispose of soiled items.

How to Prepare Her Food

I prepare some of the same foods for Ms. Julia that everyone in our family eats, but now that she cannot keep her dentures in, I mash the food or place it in a blender for a short time so that it becomes easy for her to eat. She likes to feed herself unless she is not feeling well, and then I have to feed her.

How to Give Ms. Julia Her Medicine

Once she would simply swallow pills with a cup of water, but not anymore. I have had discussions with the pharmacists, who have been quite helpful, providing instructions for mixing some of her medications with applesauce or apple butter, even using capsules that can be opened so that the medication can be stirred into the sauce. Just a few tips that work for Ms. Julia!

Saying It All with Poetry, Thoughts, and Songs!

As you read the following poetry, think about someone that you know and love who may be acting like Ms. Julia. Use Julia's story to help you decide what to do. Decide whether you can or cannot take on the responsibilities of taking care of someone like Ms. Julia. And, if you can't, it is OK! Find someone who can!

Come Back, Julia!
Come Back, Julia!

When Julia's father died, she stood strong and swallowed the
    pain.
When Julia's husband died, she stood strong, but things were
    never the same.
When Julia's oldest son died, she wept for days.
When Julia's youngest son received a fifty-nine-year jail sentence,
    her heart was broken and a part of her began to slowly die.
When Julia's one and only sister died, it was hard to tell if she
    even understood.
When her mother died, it was **hard to tell if she even
    understood**!

Come Back, Julia!

Will Alzheimer's disease have its way
With a woman who use to control her own life from day to day?

Is there just one glimmer of hope
On this slippery dementia slope,
For Julia to come back in control
Of her life, with a strong hold?

Well, I am not sure what God would say,
Since He knows her every way!
Or is it God's way of easing the pain
And just allowing His full reign
Over a life with so many struggles,
Too much for even Julia to juggle?

I know that God is in control,
For it is God and only He who saves the soul.
And since Julia knew how to pray,
And did so every day,
No matter the ups and downs,
For Julia there is a crown.

God has seen her help the needy.
He has even seen her help the greedy.
But since He really knew her heart,
From Julia, God will never depart.

Yes, Julia has come back in so many ways.
She still tries to offer help, and she still prays.
She remembers conversations with her dad,
And she remembers the good times that they had.

She doesn't remember the hurts and the pains,
And she doesn't remember the fast lanes,
Those things that hurt the most, and had such a piercing sting.
No, Julia, doesn't remember any of those things.

The Julia I know comes back every day,
Even if it's in what she does and does not say.

Vera V. Ross-Holley

Singing Makes Ms. Julia Smile

We always encourage Ms. Julia to sing, hum, and dance. While she is in the car, music blasts from the speakers the entire time; and almost always, a song comes on that she remembers. Her eyes tend to light up, and she will even hum (especially when she does not remember the words).

There is one song that Ms. Julia remembers, but she does not remember all the words, so she sings the same words over and over and over:

> *Amazing grace, how sweet the sound*
> *That saved a **wreck** [instead of **wretch**] like me.*
> *I once was lost, though now I'm found*
> *I was blind, but now I see.*
> *That saved a **wreck** like me.*
> *That saved a **wreck** like me.*
> *That saved a **wreck** like me.*

Then there are the conversations that Julia occasionally initiated:

"Holley, Has anybody seen Pretty? It's been a long time since I seen Pretty. I guess she's okay." "

Then Julia would just sit and stare as if she was really trying to make sense out of what she had just asked. As much as she loved Pretty, it must have been really hard trying to figure out just what was going on. So every now and then, Julia would ask again,

"Holley, has anybody seen Pretty? It's been a long time since I seen Pretty. I guess she's okay."

She would ask the same thing even when Pretty was sitting right in front of her. One time when she was with Pretty, Pretty responded, "This is Pretty."

Julia then asked, "Where?"

In closing, I feel that trapped in Ms. Julia's brains are memories that she often cannot recall. However, her eyes tell the story that her mouth just cannot.

The next time you see someone who acts or looks like the Julia I tried describing in this text, simply say, "Hello. How are you?"

Some will reply, and some will have a lengthy conversation with you. You may not understand the response, but you will understand the stare ... the eyes ... the heart!

What does a person with Alzheimer's disease look and act like?

Based on my experiences with Ms. Julia, my great uncle, and the many patients that I observed at long-term care facilities, and the conversations with their families, they normally look the same as they did before they became ill; however, they act very differently. Some talk excessively, while some talk a little or not at all. If they liked wearing nice clothes, many still will like dressing up in their finest outfits every day, if possible. Julia likes dressing up. I take her to consignment shops and thrift stores, where the atmosphere is not as overwhelming as that of large department stores and malls, weekly to buy clothes to replace those that she soils. The salespeople know Julia, and they know that she has Alzheimer's disease, and they are very friendly to her.

In contrast, in large department stores, the salespeople do not understand why she is asking them so many questions, why she is showing them every dress in the store, and why she talks nonstop, and asks them repeatedly, "How are you?"

Julia gets dressed up every day. When you tell her that she looks good, she responds with, "I know it! I always look good." Remember that there are, however, patients who cannot dress themselves or feed themselves. When I take Julia shopping, I let her put whatever she finds into her cart. Most of the time, by the time we get to the counter, her cart is overflowing with stuff. I just give her an empty cart and tell her to start all over again. When she goes back to shop, the salespeople (who know her) simply put the "stuff" back.

If they held certain jobs before the onset of the disease, some Alzheimer's patients will still be "living in that world," where they actually think that they are still police officers or whatever career they once enjoyed. Once a police officer, always a police officer. If they were carpenters, some will always want to fix things, even things that don't need fixing. If they cussed a lot before the disease, the cussing will continue. Wherever they are, leave them there. Let them be happy in "their own new world." Julia worked in laundries until she retired, and no one folds clothes like Julia. She knew how to make up a bed professionally, and she taught her children how to make up beds "like they do in hospitals," so every day, her job is to fold all the clothes. Nothing makes her happier; except dressing up. Julia can even fold fitted sheets, and that's something that most of us cannot do with ease. Julia also could cuss like a sailor, and she can still do that. It does not offend us; if something makes her mad, we just let her cuss.

If they were known for being quiet, polite, and dainty, this just might continue. If they were obsessive-compulsive before, they may continue being obsessive-compulsive. Julia folds everything that can be folded, even stuff that you do not want folded. She neatly piles her dishes on the table when she has finished a meal. Her clothes must match her shoes, and she has to have coffee with every meal and between meals. Some of her former life must go on. Even after drinking three cups of coffee, she will insist that no one gave her any coffee or food for the entire day.

They will not always remember the names and faces of family members. That's okay. If family members come around enough, they will begin to recognize them and expect to see them. Julia's mother passed away, and occasionally Julia would ask, "Have you seen Mother today?" My response used to be, "Julia, don't you remember? She passed away." Wrong answer, because if she had remembered that her mother had passed away, she would not have asked the question. Now, my response is, "No, I haven't seen Nanny today." When I answer that way, Julia shows no signs of confusion. With the first answer, her eyes would get really sad and then she would look totally confused.

Now, there have been times when Julia would ask, "Didn't Mother die?" My response to that now is, "Yes, she did." End of conversation. The question that was asked is answered, and there are no signs of confusion and no further questions. She does remember that her father passed away, and she will strike up the same conversation about him every time we get into a car: "Daddy asked me if I wanted to learn how to drive, and I told him, 'No, Daddy. I just want to drink.' Daddy would just break out laughing and say, 'Well, baby, I guess you won't ever drive.'" Each time after these conversations, Julia breaks out into laughter after telling this same story. The funny thing about this is that I don't get tired of hearing it.

Some Alzheimer's patients hoard things. There have been many days when our cell phones have been missing, and yes, Julia would have the phones in her underwear. The problem is that we did not know that she hid phones (initially) in her underwear until the phones rang. Just imagine trying to get a cell phone from her underwear. Well it is not an easy task because, first of all, it is very difficult getting her to pull a phone from her Depends, and second, she did not understand why we were taking her phone. If you cannot find things in your house, just look under the mattresses, or the sofa pillows, or in their bras, pockets or even in their underwear (before it's too late because the phone will need repairing if you take too long to retrieve it).

Tips for finding an alternative care facility for a loved one with Alzheimer's disease/dementia.

1. There are many long term care facilities! Visit as many as you possibly can and then you make the decision. Just remember that taking care of someone with this disease will not be easy. In Julia's case:
   - Her personality changed dramatically.
   - She has tried to fight me. There are medications for this kind of behavior. However, for Ms. Julia, I know what triggers the behavior—bathing, toileting, undressing, dressing—and I use specific strategies as detailed in this book to reduce occurrences of combative behaviors.
   - Her incontinence requires frequent underwear changes throughout the day and before she goes to bed. Julia never goes to the restroom by herself. Never! The job has not been pleasant, but it is not impossible.
   - She thrives on routine. One change in her daily routine seems to cause anxiety or confusion. She does well on schedules that do not change. However, a change here or there may be good. Remember what I said about Julia breaking her right arm?
2. There are some really great assistant living facilities even though this may be more costly.
3. Adult daycares are great, as well!
4. Whatever you decide to do, stay involved. Do not turn over full care of your loved one to others; especially strangers.

With all that said, I feel that one of the best places for a loved one with Alzheimer's disease is with a family member who knows and loves the person. Believe me, I know, because I have tried a long-term care facility and assisted living. In one facility, the staff was not even able to stop Julia from cleaning the feces from other patients.

I was absolutely appalled that her care providers did not respond appropriately to Julia's needs on many occasions. I visited almost daily, so if I was there 90 percent of the time and this facility still was not adequately taking care of Julia, just think about what would have happened if I had not been there. The thought continues to haunt me._

Visit these facilities and ask for a tour. If they cannot give you an immediate tour (within twenty-four hours), do not even consider leaving a family member there. I would not want to leave a member of my family with a facility that has to prepare for my visit.

And yes, there are some really great facilities out there. I do not want to make you think that all long-term care facilities or assisted living facilities are bad. As a matter of fact, I visited an assisted living facility that was really great. It had only two patients at the time, but the facility was clean and very cute. The bedrooms were appealing, with decorations that I felt were appropriate for Ms. Julia. The living room was comfortable, with reclining chairs for each patient. Each patient even had her own exercise equipment for daily exercises. There was a nice backyard where the residents sat in the evenings. The most important thing about this facility was that the residents seemed very happy.

You be the judge!

Now, if you decide to keep your loved one at home, some or all of my tips may help you. When it becomes very difficult, especially after a hospital stay, ask a social worker about visiting nurses, physical therapists, assistants, a hospital bed, a wheelchair, and even a portable commode. When Ms. Julia was discharged from the hospital, a social worker assisted with getting home care providers to visit on a weekly basis. There is help, and you do not have to go it alone! Ms. Julia's home care providers were excellent!

If you just want to chat, visit ComeBackJulia.com, and let's talk about it!

Hello, Doctor Jones, This is Vera, Julia
Freeman's daughter. I need to know …

Things to Know and Tell Doctors

When you notice that a family member's personality has changed, be sure to:

1. Tell the attending physician the family's medical history.
2. Tell him or her the level of alcohol consumption
3. Insist that the physicians are caring and knowledgeable. All doctors are not familiar with how to care for and treat Alzheimer's patients or patients with dementia. For everything that they prescribe, ask why.
4. Just remember that while there are some great doctors out there and that is one reason Julia is doing so well, there are just as many doctors who are not so great! Julia's current doctor takes the time to listen to my concerns and answer my questions, and he even jokes around with Julia. He does not even get mad when Julia hits him, and she hits him every time he sees her. He has asked, "Mrs. Freeman, why do you always hit me?" and she responds, "I did not hit you!" End of conversation, because Julia always wins.
5. Tell the doctor if you notice a high level of anxiety, and ask for something to manage this behavior. When stressed, Julia wants to wander, cries, and becomes totally confused. She tends to soil her clothing even more than normal when she is anxious. When Julia's anxiety is not managed, she cannot sleep at night. There have been days when Julia would sit up and not sleep at all in a forty-eight-hour period. That triggered immediate calls to her primary care provider.
6. Inform your physician if your loved one does not take his or her medication. Julia knows how to hide medication under her tongue and not swallow. Ask the physician and/ or the pharmacist about getting the same medications

in liquid form, through patches, or perhaps infusions by health care practitioners.

7. This is very important: Find a doctor who gives very specific instructions for administering medications. Ms. Julia's doctor tells me each time to try the medication and let him know how it affects her. He especially says, "If it looks like it may be causing some side effects, call me for further directions before administering the next dose." For every medication that he prescribes, he always tells me to try it first!

How I was able to tell when a doctor was not good for Julia:

A glaring indicator was when the doctor did not even touch Ms. Julia. During one visit, for example, upon entering the examining room, the assistant or nurse entered and took Julia's blood pressure. When she was unable to get Julia to stand on the scale to measure her weight, the assistant/nurse decided that she would use the measurement from Julia's recent inpatient stay. Then the doctor entered, looked at Julia, and asked about the reason for her visit. I provided some concerns (all of which were follow-up items from Julia's recent hospital stay). The doctor then walked over to Ms. Julia and attempted to touch her stomach (through her clothing), but when Ms. Julia resisted, he stopped. He did not even attempt to check her heart rate or anything else.

A second glaring indicator was when Julia was admitted to two emergency rooms three times in one week for the same symptoms, was admitted to the hospital twice, but was discharged with the same pain that she entered with, and no one knew the cause. If you want the details of this episode in Ms. Julia's life, log onto ComeBackJulia.com.

More Resources and Tips

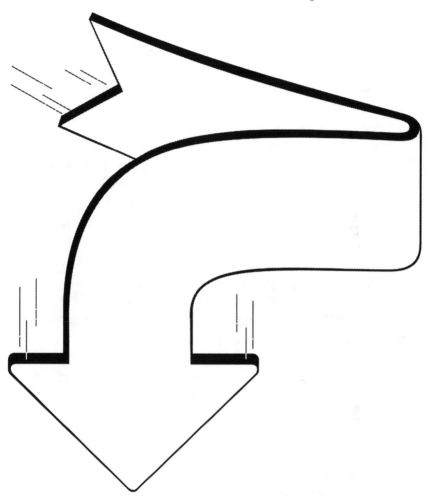

The early signs of Alzheimer's for Julia:

1. The number one sign was that Julia started losing, or not being able to manage, her money. There were times when she could not remember where she put it; and there were even more times when others had easy access to it and simply stole it. Each month for more than a year, Julia "lost" her monthly retirement and social security payments, or at least that's how the culprits described it. At some point, it did not seem to matter to her. She became totally confused because she had no control over what was happening. Her explanation was, "I don't remember where I put my money." She may not have remembered, but others did, and the monthly ritual of confusing her continued for several years.

2. Then, Julia had the strangest mood swings. She would lash out at anyone, especially those who were helping her most. She seemed to be depressed and would sit for hours in dark places, just staring into space. She was not interested in anything or anyone. It seemed as if life had been wiped out of her.

3. Hoarding came next. Julia started taking things from the neighborhood trash dumpsters and piling these things in her bedroom and in any empty spaces in her house. She had linen and other items piled up almost to the ceiling in her bedroom. She even tried hiding her money between some of these items, but would forget where she put it. (Unfortunately, others knew exactly where she put it.)

4. The disease progressed to wandering. Family members, neighbors, and friends frequently spotted Julia pushing a shopping cart filled with clothing and other items miles away from her home. There were times when she walked miles to get to her mother's house on the coldest days in the winter with just a coat, a thin dress, and sandals. Even her mother had a hard time understanding this kind of behavior. One hot summer day in Baltimore, Julia walked nine miles from Catonsville to West Baltimore

with a coat and sandals on. By the time she got to her destination, her feet were swollen and her back was blistered. She felt absolutely no pain until she reached her mother's house.

5. As the disease continued to progress, Julia would repeat the same things over and over in conversations with others. Once, her mother commented in a joking way, "This damn woman has said the same thing one hundred times!" She had a great relationship with her mother, and even if the conversations were limited, they were able to live together until it became more than her mother could manage.

6. Now, Julia does not remember the names or faces of some of her closest relatives. Occasionally, she will ask about her children, but the conversation ends just as quickly as it began. She absolutely does not remember the names of her grandchildren, friends, and other relatives. Once, she saw one of her nephews, and to our surprise (and from out of nowhere), she said, "There is Toodie!" And yes, it was Toodie, her nephew. We all began to shout in amazement. However, in the next second, she did not know who he was. This was just a glimmer of hope for those who love her.

One final note:

Never take **no** as a first answer to your questions about your loved one who is showing signs of having Alzheimer's disease. Ask more questions, or just ask another health care provider. Do not allow a doctor to intimidate you. They either know what they are doing or they do not know!

When one of Julia's physicians could not answer my questions, I found a different physician. As Julia's condition became more severe, I began taking her to specialists (a rheumatologist and a neurologist). There are some super specialists out there and some super general practitioners. You have to do the work that will lead you to the right ones. You will know which ones are right for your loved one, and you will know which ones are not.

Also, beware of the doctor who tells you repeatedly, "Well, she is getting older and there is not much we can do." Leave immediately, and get a second and maybe a third opinion. If I had listened to those doctors who said that about Julia, she probably would not have lived much longer after those statements were made. Julia is 100 percent better than she was eight years ago.

- She no longer wanders.
- She no longer smokes.
- She gets vitamins daily.
- She gets three healthy meals and snacks daily.
- She sees doctors regularly (general practitioner, podiatrist, and now a rheumatologist and a neurologist), and we ask and expect answers (the correct answers).
- She is bathed daily.
- She goes for walks with family members.
- She gets assistance with everything that she does.
- We talk to her, and we sing with her.
- We tickle her.
- We cry when she cries.
- We laugh when she laughs.
-

The journey is difficult, but so rewarding!

Thanks so much for taking this journey
with Ms. Julia!

Julia and her mother, Bernice Ross!

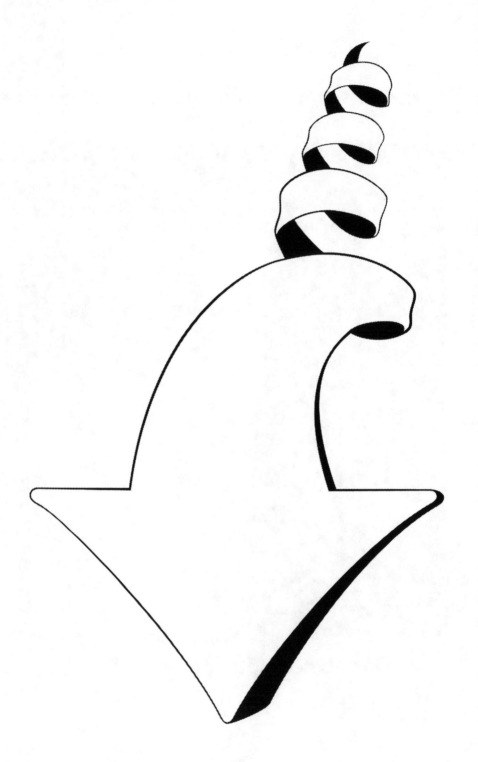

Daily Tools

Some additional tips for caregivers.

Hand Washing!

Keep a toothbrush or nail brush in all bathrooms.

Also, keep plenty of hand sanitizer in each bathroom. Carry some in your purse, as well!

I keep a toothbrush in all bathrooms because Julia scratches all the time. In the morning, for example, her nails are soiled from scratching during the night. When I get her up, I guide her straight to the bathroom so that I can clean under her nails, even before she uses the toilet. I am not sure what that stuff is under her nails in the morning, so I do not take any chances.

Ms. Julia's nails get washed in the morning (first thing), in the afternoon, in the evening, and just before she goes to bed.

Several times, she has awakened in the morning and one of her eyes has looked a little pink, and under her lower eyelash, I could tell that she had been scratching. So, maybe whatever was under her nails got into her eye.

It's time to get up, Ms. Julia, and I mean right now!

There are mornings when Ms. Julia does not want to get out of bed, but I get her up anyway. I have found that allowing her to just stay in bed all day causes her to be less alert. She has arthritis, and that makes it a little difficult getting up, but once I get her going, she is off and on her own. She has to put on her own socks and shoes, and I do not help her unless she is not feeling well. She has been doing this for so long that I do not even have to tell her which is the shoe for her right foot and which is for her left foot. She remembers.

I refuse to let her forget how to fold linen and other things, so I give her things to fold every single day, and she folds sheets perfectly.

She knows how to put on her paper underwear, put on her coat, and get water when she is thirsty.

When I see that she can do things on her own, I let her do just that!

My job is to keep Ms. Julia's brain functioning; if I do everything for her, she will forget how to do things for herself.

"Let's go, Ms. Julia. We have things to do!"

Sample Care Instructions for Julia V. Freeman
(for when she is with a sitter)

✓ Wash her face daily with Noxzema. Be careful not to get it into her eyes.

✓ At night, gently wash her face and put moisturizer on her face.

✓ Every Wednesday, soak her feet in a solution of body wash for about one hour and then dry her feet thoroughly. Use Vaseline to moisturize her feet and toes, and then put soft socks on her feet.

✓ After her bath, let her put Vaseline on her arms, legs, and hands. She will need assistance with putting Vaseline on her back. She should sleep in soft socks.

✓ Give her a multiple vitamin daily.

✓ Pour a little Ensure in her coffee (more water than coffee) four times a day on Tuesdays, Thursdays, and Saturdays.

✓ She should eat soup daily. It is okay for her to eat a whole can of soup each day: vegetable, chicken noodle, split pea, etc.

✓ She loves grilled cheese sandwiches.

✓ Give her snacks at least three times a day (bananas, canned peaches, applesauce, oranges, or graham crackers).

Always leave a care plan when someone has to sit with your loved one, even if it's only for an hour.

Sample Daily Diary Entries

If you have a family member who is showing signs of Alzheimer's disease or dementia, use the following pages to record their daily activities. The notes that you capture here will provide you with all the information that a doctor will need to diagnose the illness and to provide health care. Record everything. There is never too much information to share with a doctor. Remember: If the doctor does not appear to be listening to you, find another doctor.

Sample Diary: January 11, 2011

6:30 a.m.	Julia woke up and needed a bath because she soiled her clothing and bed linen (fully formed stool).
7:45 a.m.	Breakfast—eggs, bacon, grits, toast with jelly, coffee, and juice. Julia ate all of her food.
8:10 a.m.	Aricept and Ibuprofen—for arthritis pain (Remember that doctors always ask about medication, so keep a list of the meds.)
8:15 a.m.	Julia folded all the towels. I just give her a pile of the same towels every day.
9:00 a.m.	Medication for anxiety (Risperdone).
9:15 a.m.	Drove to the consignment shop. Julia bought a blouse.
10:00 a.m.	Doctor's appointment (geriatric specialist) for a regular check-up.
11:15 a.m.	McDonald's for lunch. Julia got a fish fillet with cheese, orange juice. We ate in.
12:20 p.m.	Back home. Julia fell asleep in the recliner and slept for two hours. Wow!
2:20 p.m.	We walked around the block, and Julia stopped to talk to everyone she met. It took us one hour and ten minutes to walk around one block.
3:30 p.m.	Julia folded towels again while I finished some paperwork. She has been feeling pretty good all day. In bed by 9:00 p.m.

These brief notes make it easier for me to keep track of Julia's good days and not so good days. When I share with her doctors, for example, I can even tell them what she ate or did not eat before she became ill or had a difficult day. When there is a problem with her bowel movements, I can refer to my notes for baseline information; for example, three bowel movements a week was normal for Julia at one time. Then, once a week became normal, but once a week concerned me, so I brought it to the attention of her doctor.

Dear Diary . . .

Starter Diary

(Begin using these pages until you purchase a notebook or diary (spiral binder, etc.)

Date: _____

_____

_____

_____

_____

_____

_____

_____

_____

_____

_____

_____

_____

_____

_____

_____

_____

_____

_____

_____

_____

_____

_____

_____

_____

_____

_____

_____

_____

Other Notes: _____
_____
_____
_____
_____

Starter Diary

Date: _____
_____
_____
_____
_____
_____
_____
_____
_____
_____
_____
_____
_____
_____
_____
_____
_____
_____
_____

Other Notes: _____
_____
_____
_____

Starter Diary

Date: _____

Other Notes: _____

Starter Diary

Date: _____

_____

_____

_____

_____

_____

_____

_____

_____

_____

_____

_____

_____

_____

_____

_____

_____

_____

_____

_____

Other Notes: _____

_____

_____

_____

_____

_____

_____

Starter Diary

Date: _____

_____
_____
_____
_____
_____
_____
_____
_____
_____
_____
_____
_____
_____
_____
_____
_____
_____
_____
_____

Other Notes: _____

_____
_____
_____
_____
_____
_____

Starter Diary

Date: _____

_____

_____

_____

_____

_____

_____

_____

_____

_____

_____

_____

_____

_____

_____

_____

_____

_____

_____

_____

Other Notes: _____

_____

_____

_____

_____

_____

_____

Starter Diary

Date: _____

_____

_____

_____

_____

_____

_____

_____

_____

_____

_____

_____

_____

_____

_____

_____

_____

_____

_____

_____

Other Notes: _____

_____

_____

_____

_____

_____

_____

Starter Diary

Date: _____

_____

_____

_____

_____

_____

_____

_____

_____

_____

_____

_____

_____

_____

_____

_____

_____

_____

_____

_____

_____

Other Notes: _____

_____

_____

_____

_____

_____

_____

Starter Diary

Date: _____

_____

_____

_____

_____

_____

_____

_____

_____

_____

_____

_____

_____

_____

_____

_____

_____

_____

_____

_____

_____

_____

Other Notes: _____

_____

_____

_____

_____

_____

_____

Starter Diary

Date: _____

_____

_____

_____

_____

_____

_____

_____

_____

_____

_____

_____

_____

_____

_____

_____

_____

_____

_____

_____

Other Notes: _____

_____

_____

_____

_____

_____

Starter Diary

Date: _____

_____

_____

_____

_____

_____

_____

_____

_____

_____

_____

_____

_____

_____

_____

_____

_____

_____

_____

Other Notes: _____

_____

_____

_____

_____

_____

Communication works!

Sample Written Communications to Those Who Have Provided Care for Julia

Get in the habit of providing feedback to those who are charged with caring for your loved-one (good, bad, or indifferent—say what needs to be said).

Sample Letter No. 1

Vera V. Holley
(for Julia V. Freeman)
3924 Sadie Road
Randallstown, MD 21133
443-271-7362

June 29, 2009

President and COO
Northwest Hospital
Old Court Road
Randallstown, MD 21133

Dear Sir,

I was most impressed with the professionalism of Northwest Hospital's staff when my mother, Julia Freeman, was admitted for a fractured pelvic bone. The high level of attentiveness to her needs was commendable. My mother's dementia and confusion did not present a problem to those who were in charge of her care. At one time, it seemed like my mother was the only patient in the hospital. I was thrilled at the level of care provided for her. Her immediate care nurse treated her with the most respect by addressing her as "Ms. Julia."

I am so thankful for the many caring staff members at Northwest who provided such great care for my mother.

Sincerely,
Vera V. Holley

Vera V. Holley
(for Julia V. Freeman)
3924 Sadie Road
Randallstown, MD 21133
443-271-7362

June 29, 2009

Administrator
FutureCare Old Court
5412 Old Court Road
Randallstown, MD 21133

Dear Sir,

I was very impressed with the professionalism of Future Care Old Court's staff while my mother, Julia V. Freeman, was a resident there after fracturing her pelvic bone. The transition from Northwest Hospital to Future Care was expedited in a highly professional manner and this reduced my anxiety and especially my mother's anxiety. I was very comfortable leaving my mother in the care of the staff at Future Care.

I was most impressed with my mother's immediate care provider, who treated her like she was a member of his own family. He is one of the most caring people I have ever met. He made an extra effort to get to know her and to implement the individualized care plan offered at Future Care. I knew immediately after watching him care for my mother and her roommate that my mother was safe and very comfortable with him. The quality of care that he provided for my mother compared to the personal care that I provide for her. I simply could not have asked for anything more than that.

In addition to the personal care provider, the nursing staff and physical therapist were knowledgeable, friendly, attentive, and genuinely concerned about my mother's care; and from my observations, each patient was given the same high level of care. The attentiveness of the staff is the highest I have ever witnessed in a long-term care facility. Each time I visited the facility, nurses and other staff members were always close at hand. There was an overall "community" feel that was present the moment I walked in the front door, where the receptionists also presented themselves in a highly professional manner.

Sincerely yours,
Vera V. Holley

Vera V. Holley
(for Julia V. Freeman)
3924 Sadie Road
Randallstown, MD 21133
443-271-7362

April 13, 2011

The Home Health Care Provider
Baltimore, MD 21244

To Whom It May Concern,

I am sending this letter for two reasons. One reason is to give accolades to the nurse who visited my mother on a weekly basis and was responsible for taking care of a wound on the side of her hip, ordering supplies, making sure that my mother's health needs were met, and offering advice. My mother had become quite familiar and comfortable with the nurse. At the end of each visit, my mother would hug her and smile. When a lab tech at a local facility was not able to draw blood from my mother for lab work, the nurse not only made arrangements to draw the blood, but did so without any complications. She and I had a routine for taking care of my mother's wound, and because of that, the wound began healing quite rapidly. The nurse checked my mother's vitals each visit, and checked to make sure that she had adequate supplies, and that her medications were effective.

I also want to say that I was extremely satisfied with the physical therapist who significantly impacted my mother's quick recovery from what appeared to be severe immobility. She was quite knowledgeable about my mother's condition, and she was quite capable of initiating and following through with measures to help my mother recover. My mother loves the hospital bed and wheelchair that the physical therapist ordered for her. Once in bed, she falls asleep and does not wake up until the next morning. The wheelchair that was ordered especially for my mother based on her height and weight makes it much easier for her to get around.

In closing, I hope that this letter will serve as supportive feedback that can be used to inform decisions related to home care for patients with dementia. Many thanks for helping me to take care of Ms. Julia.

Sincerely,
Vera V. Holley
shugholley@comcast.net

Log onto ComeBackJulia.com for access to a letter that expressed serious concerns about how Julia was treated by her primary care provider and the attending staff of two hospitals.

Now, it's time for Ms. Julia to go to bed . . .

"Julia, are you ready for bed?"
Julia replies, "Hell no!"
That's my Julia!